D1453193

PERSONAL MANAGEMENT

By Brent A. Neiser, CFP
National Endowment for Financial Education

BOY SCOUTS OF AMERICA
IRVING, TEXAS

Requirements

1. Do the following:

    a. Lead a discussion with your family to identify one family financial goal that must be saved for out of family income. Choose a goal that has strong personal interest for both you and your family (a family trip or vacation, a new VCR, or a family car, for instance).

    b. Discuss the goal in detail (where to go on vacation, for example, or what kind of car to buy), the cost of the goal, and when you want to reach the goal.

    c. Discuss how your family could accumulate funds to reach this goal, how the goal will affect the rest of the family budget, and how you could help your family achieve the goal.

2. Do the following:

    a. Prepare a personal budget or spending plan for three months, including a "pay yourself first" savings plan. Keep track of everything you buy. Balance all income with expenses and savings at the end of each month.

    b. Share your three-month budget with your merit badge counselor. Explain how you determined discretionary income (income not spent to meet fixed expenses), how much you saved, and what you spent money on. Did you spend more or less than you budgeted?

3. Do ONE of the following:

    a. Identify a personal financial goal and make a plan to achieve that goal.

35002
ISBN 0-8395-5002-2
© 1996 Boy Scouts of America
2000 Printing of the 1996 Edition

(1) Write down the goal you want to achieve. (This may be a small, short-term goal such as buying clothes, or it may be a major, long-term goal such as saving for college.)

(2) Develop a financial plan to accomplish the goal. Determine how much the goal will cost, how much time you have to reach the goal, how you will earn money to pay for the goal, and what adjustments you could make if you cannot reach the goal in the desired time with the income you can earn.

(3) Discuss your plan with your counselor.

OR:

b. Determine a spending/savings plan for living on your own.

(1) Choose a realistic job based on your age, skills, education, and experience (working at a fast-food restaurant, movie theater, or college library, for example). Determine how much you would probably make per hour and how many hours you would work each week. Determine your spendable income (after taxes and other deductions are taken out) for a month.

(2) Make a list of all basic monthly living expenses: rent, food, transportation, clothing, telephone, etc. Ask family or friends, or call sources to help determine costs.

(3) Compare projected income with projected expenses. Would you have enough income to live on? Would any be left over for fun? For savings?

(4) If expenses exceed income, determine what options you would have for bringing the two into balance. Could you reduce or eliminate expenses? Work more hours a week? Get a higher-paying job?

(5) Discuss your final plan with your counselor.

4. Do the following:

a. Choose an item you would like to buy. Be specific. (For example, identify the brand name of a pair of shoes you want, or the title of a CD.)

b. Comparison shop for the item. Find out where you can buy the item for the best price. Call around; study ads. Look for a sale or a discount coupon.

c. Consider alternatives. Could you buy the item used? Should you wait for a sale?

d. Discuss your shopping strategy with your counselor.

5. Do ONE of the following:

a. Visit a bank. Ask a bank representative to explain checking accounts, savings accounts, loans, and automated teller machines (ATMs). Explain to your counselor the difference between a checking account and a savings account. Discuss with your counselor the minimum requirements to open and maintain the accounts or to take out a loan.

OR:

b. Visit another type of financial institution, such as a stock brokerage firm or an insurance company. Ask a representative what the firm does and how it works with consumers. Explain to your counselor the differences in services offered by the following types of financial professionals: financial planner, stockbroker, insurance agent, accountant, tax preparer, banker, estate planning attorney.

6. Do the following:

a. Explain the difference between saving for a goal and investing for a goal.

b. Explain the two basic methods of investing: loaned and owned.

c. Explain the concepts of simple and compound interest and how compound interest can be used to increase your savings and investments more rapidly.

d. Explain the concepts of yield, profit, and total return, and how they are used to evaluate investment performance.

e. Explain the basic features of the following types of investments, including risks and rewards and whether they involve lending or owning: bank savings accounts, certificates of deposit, U.S. Savings Bonds, shares of stock, shares in a mutual fund, real estate.

4

7. Do the following:

   a. Explain what a loan is, what interest is, and how the "annual percentage rate" measures the true cost of a loan.

   b. Choose something that you want to buy or do, but currently cannot afford. Set up an imaginary loan so you can "achieve" that goal. Identify the "principal" amount, interest rate, and repayment schedule. Determine the total cost of the loan (principal plus interest). Determine how it would affect your total cost if you paid back the same amount every two weeks instead of once a month.

   c. Explain the differences between a charge card, a debit card, and a credit card.

   d. Identify the factors that affect the costs of credit. Tell which factors can be controlled.

   e. Explain credit reports and how personal responsibility can affect your credit record.

   f. Describe ways to reduce or eliminate debt.

8. Do the following:

   a. Explain the five ways to manage risk.

   b. Explain the six basic types of insurance and why someday you might need one or more of them.

   c. Define the two major types of life insurance (term and permanent) and compare their advantages and disadvantages.

9. Do the following:

   a. Identify a job or career that interests you and do basic research about it at your library or through other information sources. Make a presentation to your troop or counselor about the job or career. Your report should include:

      (1) An explanation of your interest in the job or career (how you learned of it, what about it that interests you, what its job prospects are, and how you think the job or career will change in the future)

      (2) Any qualifications required (education, skills, experiences) and how you might become qualified for the job

    (3) The job's functions and responsibilities (the duties of the job or career)

    (4) The organizations, trade associations, professional associations, governmental regulations, or licenses involved in the career field

b. Do ONE of the following:

    (1) Prepare a personal résumé for the job.

OR:

    (2) Interview someone in the job or career field and prepare a summary of the interview.

c. Discuss with your counselor your personal goals and ambitions in life. Relate these to your intellectual, physical, spiritual, and moral development. How has Scouting helped you in accomplishing your goals and ambitions? Share your thoughts with your family.

Contents

1

Managing Yourself

"Personal management" sounds important, doesn't it? But maybe you're not quite sure what it means. *Personal management* is taking responsibility for yourself and your own actions—it means taking control of your life.

"Hey, I've always wanted to be in charge of my own life," you might be saying. Most young people, especially teenagers, want to have more control over their lives. That's a healthy attitude. It's a natural part of growing up. It helps young people become responsible adults.

But managing yourself can also be a little scary. It means no longer depending on others as much to do things or make decisions for you. It means being responsible for your own mistakes, as well as your own successes.

Think of all the things your parents or other adults do for you. Do the adults in your life buy and prepare your food, put a roof over your head and clothes on your back, drive you to places you want to go, and help pay for things you want to buy or do? What if you had to do all of those things for yourself?

You're probably used to having others manage much of your life for you. Your parents or guardians tell you what to do, your teachers tell you what to learn, your coaches tell you how to play a sport. You might not always agree with what they tell you, but you probably realize it's their way of teaching the skills and knowledge you'll need when you are grown and truly on your own.

As you're growing up, however, you start to take more responsibility for yourself. That's what this merit badge is about. Earning the Personal Management merit badge will help you learn to better manage three critical parts of your life: your money, your time, and your future.

You're not entirely on your own yet, and you won't be until you're old enough to move away from home. You still share the management of your life with adults. But now is a good time to prepare yourself for the day you leave home. It's like taking flying lessons for the big day when you finally get to pilot the plane solo.

2

Managing Your Money

Learning to manage money is a skill that has become more important—and more difficult—than it was when your parents were growing up. Your parents and grandparents probably had less money as teenagers than many teens do today, and they certainly had fewer items to spend money on. Today's teenagers face more complicated choices than people once did about how to earn money, save it, and spend it. Young people today must be more responsible for their own financial futures, such as saving for retirement. And because people today have more choices, they also have more chances to make financial mistakes, such as getting too deeply into debt.

Of course, money isn't and shouldn't be everything in life. There are far more important things, like family, friends, helping others, and achieving personal growth. But money is a major part of life for most people. How a person manages money is critical to his or her personal, and perhaps even family's, well-being. The main purpose of responsible money management is not to make more money, although that can sometimes be helpful and necessary. Rather, the goal is to wisely and effectively manage the money you do have.

Money-management habits—good or bad—are not something people are born with. We learn these habits, particularly when we are young.

Bad money-management habits often affect people's relationships with other people. Conflicts over money can cause stress in families and marriages. Disputes about money are among the leading causes of divorce.

Conflicts over finances occur most often among people who don't know how to successfully manage their money. What you learn while completing this merit badge about earning, saving, and spending your money wisely can serve you for a lifetime.

3

Meeting a Family Financial Goal

People seek money for two basic reasons: to provide for their needs and to satisfy their wants.

Needs are what people require for survival: food, clothing, shelter, and medical care, for example. When you are preparing for a campout, you make sure you have the things you need to survive in the outdoors.

Wants are the things people desire to make life more comfortable or enjoyable, or because friends have them, or because they are symbols of power, or simply because they're appealing.

Sometimes it's difficult to tell the difference between needs and wants. Clothing is a need, but expensive designer clothes are not. A car might be necessary for getting to work, but it doesn't have to be an expensive new car—that's a want.

Young people your age have many wants, and tend to buy such things as CDs, baseball cards, jewelry, or computer games. On the other hand, you might also contribute money toward your family's needs, such as food, shelter, or your own clothing.

Understanding the difference between needs and wants wouldn't be so important except for one thing: Most people don't have enough money to buy *everything* they need *and* want. Usually a person or a family has a limited amount of income available to spend each month. For example, you probably can spend only what you receive from your allowance or what you earn from a job.

Goals and Objectives

Few people have an unlimited income. Most people must make important decisions about how to spend money. A family, for example, must first take care of needs, such as paying for food and housing. What's left over can then be saved or spent on wants.

A good way to make decisions about spending money, especially for wants, is to develop goals and objectives.

A *goal* is a specific purpose or destination. Goals are dreams and wishes brought to reality. "Gee, I hope our school band can travel out of state sometime to play" is a wish or dream. "Our school band is going to play in the Rose Bowl Parade in Pasadena in January" is a goal. It has a specific destination and time. It is concrete. It is something everyone in the band can work toward.

Achieving a goal requires setting *objectives*. Objectives are the details—the tasks and steps required to accomplish the goal. Sending the band to the Rose Bowl Parade will require money. One objective could be for each student to earn a specific amount for the trip. The students could earn extra money on their own and they could work together on group fund-raising projects.

Having clear, specific goals is a key to managing money well. When people don't have goals, they tend to waste money. They don't know exactly where their money went or why. Setting goals, in fact, is a key to managing many aspects of life well. As the famous baseball player Yogi Berra once said, "If you don't know where you are going, you'll probably end up someplace else."

While you have your own goals, your family probably has goals, too. Many of these goals will require money. For example, your family might want to buy a car or television, get out of debt, go on a vacation, or move to a different apartment.

Suppose the family goal is to go on a vacation. Whether it is a long, expensive vacation far from home or a short, inexpensive trip to a nearby spot, the decisions you must make are basically the same.

First, you must decide where you would like to go and when. What would interest the entire family? It might be visiting relatives in the next state or traveling across the country to the Grand Canyon.

Next, you must decide how you will get there. By car? Bus? Plane? Train? This decision might depend on several factors: how far you'll be traveling, how much time you have, how you like to travel, and how much each type of travel will cost.

You must decide where you will stay when you get there. With friends or relatives? In a motel or condominium? In an RV or a tent?

And what will you do while you're there? That decision will depend on your family's interests, how much time you will have, and how much activities will cost.

By discussing these things, the family can mutually agree on important decisions. Once you know where you're going and when, how you'll get there, where and how long you'll stay, and what you'll do while you're there, then you've set a specific goal. Next you can

take the first steps to accomplish your goal by making the necessary arrangements (such as reserving a motel room) and saving the money to pay for the trip.

You can use this same approach no matter what the family goal is. If you want to buy a television, for example, you'll have to make decisions about screen size and other features you want, and how much you can afford to pay.

Reaching Goals

After setting a specific goal, your family should discuss how it will save enough money to reach that goal. If the goal is a vacation trip, discuss what impact such a trip will have on your family's overall finances. Can the vacation be paid for out of regular income? Or will your family need to save extra money? Perhaps a special vacation fund will need to be set up. If your family wants to leave in six months, divide the estimated cost of the vacation by six. Then you'll know exactly how much money must be saved each month.

How can you help your family reach its goal? Perhaps you could earn extra money by mowing neighbors' lawns or shoveling snow from their sidewalks. Perhaps you could get a part-time or temporary job.

Or your family might need to cut back on expenses. Maybe you've wanted a new pair of athletic shoes. By not buying those shoes right now, your family could use that money for the vacation instead. That's often what reaching goals is about: trading one want for another.

Sometimes, despite a family's best efforts, it won't be able to save enough money to pay for a goal as planned. In the case of the vacation, for example, your family might have to reconsider where it wants to go, how it will get there, how long to stay, or what to do while there.

4

Making and Following a Personal Spending and Savings Plan

How about setting a personal goal—a goal just for yourself? You can follow the same process used to reach a family goal.

First, identify the goal. It might be a small, short-term goal such as buying clothes, a gift for a friend, concert tickets, or a video game. Or it might be a more expensive, long-term goal such as saving for a Scout trip, a computer, or a college education.

Find out how much the goal will cost. That's usually easy to determine. You could go window-shopping or read newspaper ads to find the average price of a CD or how much a computer costs, for example.

Sometimes, however, it's easy to underestimate the cost. Suppose you're old enough to drive and you want to buy your own car. You might know what car you want to buy and its price. But have you thought about how much it will cost to operate the car once you've bought it? Will you have enough money for gas and oil, insurance, repairs, license plates, registration fees, and the other expenses involved in maintaining a car?

Once you know what your goal will cost, determine how much time you have in which to reach the goal. Is your friend's birthday next week? Is the start of college two years away? Calculate how much you need to save in the next week, or each month, to reach your goal.

How to Save Money

To achieve a financial goal, you must save enough money to pay for the goal (unless you use credit to cover the cost; credit is discussed later in the section on managing debt). To save enough, you need to earn or receive income and then regularly set aside enough of your income to reach your goal.

You probably can think of several sources of income. Here are a few ideas.

- **Allowance.** You might receive a weekly or monthly allowance, perhaps in return for doing certain chores.

- **Extra chores.** Maybe you could do extra chores around the house for extra income. You could earn money and probably save your busy parents valuable time.

- **Gifts.** Save gifts of money that you receive for birthdays, Christmas, a bar mitzvah, or other special occasions.

- **Job.** Perhaps you could work at a local fast-food restaurant or movie theater, deliver papers or distribute fliers, or work as a golf caddy.

- **Your own business.** You might create your own jobs. Have you ever considered house-sitting, pet care for neighbors, computer instruction, tutoring, operating a messenger service, repairing bikes, or running errands for elderly neighbors? Business opportunities are limited only by your imagination and determination.

- **Selling something.** You might raise money by selling something you own that you no longer want, such as baseball cards or an old bike.

Budgeting

Receiving money from these or other sources is only half of what you need to do to reach your goal. You also must save some of that money. Saving is not always easy to do. You might have other things you want or need to spend your money on, such as clothing, music, movies and other entertainment, contributions to church, Scout dues, candy and snacks, and school lunches. If you spend all of your income on those things, you won't have anything left over for your goal.

This is where a personal spending/savings plan comes in. A personal spending/savings plan, often called a *budget,* organizes your finances to show you what income you are receiving, how you plan to spend it, and how you actually spend it. Most people—adults included—hate budgets. People usually think of a budget as something that tells them what they *can't* spend. But a budget can actually help you plan how you *can* spend your money wisely.

One of the requirements for this merit badge calls for preparing and keeping a personal spending/savings plan for three months. The next page shows a sample plan.

Income

	Month 1		Month 2		Month 3		Total	
	Planned	Actual	Planned	Actual	Planned	Actual	Planned	Actual
Allowance	$20	$_____	$20	$_____	$20	$_____	$ 60	$_____
Job	$50	$_____	$50	$_____	$50	$_____	$150	$_____
Gifts	$20	$_____	$ 0	$_____	$ 0	$_____	$ 20	$_____
Other	$ 0	$_____	$ 0	$_____	$10	$_____	$ 10	$_____
Totals	$90	$_____	$70	$_____	$80	$_____	$240	$_____

Expenses

	Month 1		Month 2		Month 3		Total	
	Planned	Actual	Planned	Actual	Planned	Actual	Planned	Actual
Savings	$25	$_____	$25	$_____	$25	$_____	$ 75	$_____
Church	$ 7	$_____	$ 7	$_____	$ 7	$_____	$ 21	$_____
Scout dues	$ 4	$_____	$ 4	$_____	$ 4	$_____	$ 12	$_____
Snacks	$10	$_____	$10	$_____	$10	$_____	$ 30	$_____
Gifts	$ 6	$_____	$ 6	$_____	$14	$_____	$ 26	$_____
Entertainment	$10	$_____	$20	$_____	$10	$_____	$ 40	$_____
Miscellaneous	$12	$_____	$12	$_____	$12	$_____	$ 36	$_____
Totals	$74	$_____	$84	$_____	$82	$_____	$240	$_____

To make a budget like this work, you must keep track of all of your income and expenses. At the end of each day—just before bed, perhaps—write down any income you received and expenses you paid. Be as exact as possible. Even small amounts, like 25 cents, add up over a month. You might write down each item in a notebook with the date, and then add up everything under its correct category at the end of each month.

If you have a job or get an allowance, it's pretty easy to predict what income you'll receive for the month. However, be careful not to count income you're not sure you will receive.

It's not always easy to estimate exactly what your expenses will be. Some expenses, such as your savings, Scout dues, and church donations, are usually "fixed," which means they are the same every month. You also might know the exact cost of a one-time expense such as a gift for a friend. But it's more difficult to predict exactly what you'll spend on "wants" such as snacks or entertainment.

Ideally, total expenses should be equal to or less than total income for the month. Any money left over at the end of the month can be added to savings or kept to spend next month. If you spend more than you budgeted in one category, such as movies, you should adjust for it by spending less in another category, such as snacks.

If you spend more than your total income for the month, you will have to borrow money and then pay it back next month. Borrowing will be discussed later.

Pay Yourself First

Notice in the sample spending/savings plan that "savings" comes first in the expense section. One of the tricks of saving toward a goal is to "pay yourself first." Say you want to save $15 each month. Put the first $15 of income for the month in an envelope or a savings account (savings accounts will be discussed later in the section on financial institutions).

Then you can spend your remaining income on other expenses. Of course, you want to be sure you have enough to pay for "fixed" expenses such as church contributions or car payments. The expenses you have left are "discretionary" expenses. Those are the things you don't necessarily *have* to spend money on, such as movies or candy.

What happens if you budget the other way around—that is, you don't save until last? It's likely you will find you don't have enough left at the end of the month to put the budgeted amount into savings. Thus, you won't be able to meet your goal.

How much should you save? One good rule is to save at least 10 percent of your total income. If you can save 20 percent to 30 percent, that's even better.

Budgets often need adjusting. Maybe you don't have enough income to cover all your expenses. What changes can you make? One option is to find ways to earn more money. You also could look for ways to cut expenses. You might decide that changing the amount of your church donations or Scout dues is not an option, but you might be able to spend less on movies, candy, or other discretionary expenses.

Another option is to change your goal. Perhaps you will need more time to save the necessary money. Or you might decide to save for a less expensive goal (for example, to buy a less expensive bike than the one you originally wanted).

The advantage of a budget is that it shows you clearly what choices you have, and what changes you could make to achieve your goal.

5

On Your Own

Earlier, "personal management" was defined as taking responsibility for yourself. As you get older, you learn to shoulder more and more responsibility. At the moment, your parents or another adult might be generally responsible for you. They may take care of most of your needs and, perhaps, many of your wants.

Suppose, however, that you lived on your own. That will happen someday soon, possibly when you enter college or when you and your family decide you are old enough to get out on your own. That probably sounds exciting. All young people want to grow up. But with this new freedom will come new responsibilities. Suddenly you will have expenses that have always been paid by someone else: food, a place to live, utilities, cable television, a telephone, and personal items. You won't be able to spend your money only on fun things. Good money management will become critical.

How much would it cost to live on your own? You can get an idea by drawing up an imaginary spending/savings plan.

Income and Expenses

First, to live on your own, you need to have a steady job. You no longer can depend on an allowance or other support from your family. Choose a realistic job based on your age, skills, education, and experience. For a teenager, this might mean working at a fast-food restaurant, movie theater, or college library, or as an unskilled construction worker.

Choose a job. Find out what such a job pays hourly and how many hours you might work a week. From this, calculate your *take-home pay* for one month. That's the money you will have left after your employer takes out payroll deductions for taxes, Social Security, and possibly other deductions such as health insurance. In essence, take-home pay is the money you have left to spend. If your job pays $6 an hour, you might be able to take home only $4 or $4.50 an hour.

Next, decide what you need out of your monthly take-home pay to live on. Add up *all* of your basic monthly living expenses. The list provided here can serve as a guide. To estimate expenses, talk to your parents and Scout leader, or make phone calls. Go with someone to the grocery store to see what a week's worth of food for you would cost. Calculate how much gas for a week would cost.

There are lots of expenses when you live on your own, aren't there? How do your estimated expenses compare with your estimated income? Would you have enough income to live on?

If estimated expenses are greater than estimated income, what adjustments could you make? You could try to find a higher-paying job. But that's not always easy, especially if you don't have the right education or skills. You could work more hours. Some adults work two or three jobs to make ends meet. But if you're in school, that means you would have fewer hours to devote to schoolwork. And education is vital to getting higher-paying jobs.

As you did with your budget earlier, look for ways to reduce expenses. Perhaps you could share an apartment with a friend to cut the cost of rent. You could take the bus or subway instead of owning a car. You might decide to cut back what you spend on eating out or on entertainment. That's not much fun, of course, but sometimes people must do things they would rather not do. That's part of personal management.

Basic Living Expenses

Expense	Amount
Savings	$ _____
Rent	_____
Groceries	_____
Eating out	_____
Utilities	_____
Telephone	_____
Personal grooming	_____
Car/transportation (gas, license, parking, bus fare)	_____
Clothing/laundry	_____
Insurance	_____
Medical care	_____
Church/charities	_____
Entertainment (cable TV, movies, dating)	_____
CDs, tapes, etc.	_____
Recreation	_____
Sports/hobbies	_____
Vacations	_____
Books, magazines	_____
Gifts	_____
Miscellaneous (items not covered by other categories)	_____
Total monthly expenses	$ _____

Being a Smart Shopper

You know how to spend money, right? You walk into a store, pick out what you want, hand the clerk enough money to pay for the item, and it's yours. That's easy.

But did you know there are some tricks that will make the money you spend go further? What if you could have paid less for exactly the same item, or a similar item, at another store? Or suppose you had a discount coupon that allowed you to buy the item for less than its regular price? Then you would have money left over to save for the future or to spend on something else you need or want. Every time you save money shopping, it's as though you earned that same amount.

Suppose you have your eye on a really special skateboard. How much does it cost? (Don't forget to include the cost of protective gear if you don't already own such items.) You count your money and discover that you don't have enough. What do you do? You might:

- Shop around. Maybe another store or a catalog has the identical skateboard at a cheaper price. A telephone can make comparison shopping easy. Call at least three stores.

- Earn or save more money until you have enough to buy the skateboard.

- Wait for a sale. A store clerk might tell you if the skateboard will go on sale soon.

- Look for discount coupons. These can be found in newspapers, coupon books, or the mail.

What if you still don't have enough money to buy the skateboard, or you decide you don't want to spend that much money, even if it is on sale? You have other choices. Shoppers can't always buy exactly what they want. Sometimes they must compromise. That's part of being a good money manager—knowing when to say no to yourself.

In the case of the skateboard, you could

- Buy a less expensive skateboard. Maybe the paint job or design isn't what you originally wanted, but you can still have a lot of fun on the skateboard.

- Buy a used skateboard from a friend, at a garage sale, or at a store that sells used sporting equipment.

- Check newspaper classified ads.

- Build your own skateboard. Not only would that save money, it also would be a fun project. And because you built it, you probably would value it more.

Other Shopping Tips

Here are more tips for smart shopping:

- Be wary of advertising. Advertising messages bombard you daily. Advertising serves many useful purposes. It tells you what products are available to buy, their features and benefits, who's selling the products, and often at what cost. But advertising can be misleading, too. The package might say "new and improved." But how is it improved? It might be only a small change that makes no real difference in the overall quality or features of the product. Does the product really deliver the benefits that are claimed or suggested? Ask yourself: "Will that pair of athletic shoes being promoted by my favorite basketball player really help me jump higher?"

- Before buying a product, talk to friends, family members, or others who may already use or own the product. Do they like it? Was it worth what they paid for it?

- Try a product before buying. Rent a video game or play it at a friend's house before buying to be sure it's what you want. Have a salesperson give a demonstration of the product. Test-drive a car you think you want to buy and compare it with other cars.

- Consider quality. Price isn't everything. Check the local library for consumer guides on product price, quality, and value. Why buy something, even at a low price, if it falls apart quickly or doesn't work properly?

- Consider service. A store might offer a great price but it might not offer friendly or competent repair service or a guarantee if there is a problem with the product.

- Consider features. Do you really need the latest (and usually most expensive) computer or all those features on a stereo system?

- Avoid impulse buying. That is, don't buy something without taking the time to consider whether you really need or want the item, or whether you can buy it somewhere else for less. Impulse buying often occurs when you're planning to buy one item and something else catches your eye.

- If there's a problem, take a product back right away (be sure to keep your receipt). Don't toss the item aside and feel sorry for yourself. Tell a store representative the problem. Most stores don't want to sell defective products. They'll probably fix the item or give you a new one.

7

Visiting a Financial Institution

There's an old joke—which some people believe is true—that a checking account is not overdrawn until the checkbook runs out of checks. If you have opened and used a checking account at a bank, you might understand the humor of this joke (if not, it will be explained later). Many people, adults included, who use banks and other financial institutions every day do not fully understand how financial institutions work, the services offered, or which institutions and services fit their needs.

People often don't understand the differences between a bank, a savings and loan, and a credit union (the differences are fewer today than in the past). Many misunderstandings also exist about the differences between a bank and other types of financial institutions such as a brokerage firm.

Banks are the most commonly used of all financial institutions. Visit your local bank and look at ways it can help you manage your money.

When you walk into a bank, one of the first things you'll probably see is a row of people behind a long counter. These bank employees are called tellers or customer service representatives. They help customers deposit (put in) or withdraw (take out) money, write checks, or get into safe-deposit boxes. (A bank customer can rent a safe-deposit box, located inside a bank vault, in which to safely store important papers and valuables like jewelry.) Another part of the bank will have desks where representatives can help you open a checking or savings account, take out a loan, or make investments.

Savings Account

One of the first things many teenagers do at a bank is to open a *savings account*. A savings account is not unlike a piggy bank you might have kept at home. It's where you save money for a rainy day or for one of your goals. It's smart to have a savings account once you begin earning or receiving money.

What Is Money?

Money is a "medium of exchange." If someone sells you something, you give that person money. In turn, that person can use the money to buy something from someone else.

Using money generally is easier than *bartering*. Bartering is a direct exchange of goods or services (trading). Maybe you've traded a baseball card for another baseball card (or maybe one card for several cards). That's bartering. But bartering gets complicated when more than two people are involved, or if one person doesn't have what the other person wants. Maybe your friend doesn't have the baseball card you want to trade for. Then your friend might pay you money for your card, and you could use that money to buy the card you want from someone else.

Strictly speaking, money has no value itself. A dollar bill is simply paper with printing on it. Its only value lies in how much it will buy in exchange.

Throughout history, money has come in many forms: elephant hair, seashells, whale teeth, cattle, gold and silver, and paper. As recently as the 1940s, Yap Islanders in the western Pacific Ocean used huge, heavy stone wheels as a sign of their wealth.

Keeping your cash in a savings account at a bank rather than in a piggy bank or stuffed under your mattress is smart for several reasons:

- A thief might take your money at home. Money kept at a bank is insured by the federal government against loss or theft.

- A fire or other natural disaster could destroy your money at home.

- The bank will pay you money, called interest, on the money you deposit in a savings account. The bank pays you interest because you are actually loaning the bank money, which it in turn loans to other customers. (How interest works is explained later in the section on investing.) Money you leave sitting in a piggy bank or stuffed under a mattress earns nothing.

Checking Account

As you earn more money and begin paying bills, such as insurance payments on a car, you'll probably want to open a *checking account* so you can write checks. (In most cases, you can't write checks on a savings account.)

What is a check? Think of it as a note telling your bank how much money to take out of your account and give to the person or company (the *payee*) to whom you wrote the check. The bank gives the payee that amount in cash, or electronically transfers that amount from your checking account to the payee's bank account.

Of course, for the bank to withdraw money from your checking account to compensate the payee, you must have put money into your account. Typically, you put money into a checking account by depositing cash or a check written by someone else, such as an employer.

Checks are a convenient way to pay bills, such as rent or auto insurance. Writing a check also can be safer than carrying around a large amount of cash, which could more easily be lost or stolen.

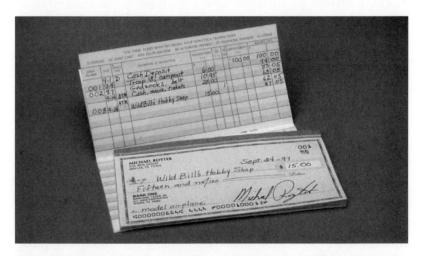

Be sure to deduct any per-item charges, service charges, or ATM fees. When applicable, add any interest earned. Be sure to record all automated (pre-authorized) payments/deposits on the date scheduled.

Having a checking account requires keeping good records. When you run out of cash, you know it. But it can be easy to *overdraw* a checking account and not realize right away that you have overdrawn it. Remember the joke earlier about the checking account being overdrawn only when the checkbook runs out of checks? Actually, a checking account is overdrawn when you write checks that total more than the amount you have deposited in your account. In fact, a single check can overdraw an account.

Some banks pay interest on checking accounts, much like a savings account, but generally they charge a fee for the checking service. That's because it costs banks money to process checks. Banks typically offer different types of checking accounts. Fees can be based on how much money you keep in your account, how many checks you write a month, and so on.

Other Services

Banks also *loan* money. They loan money to customers who agree to pay the money back, plus interest, at a later date. (Loans will be explained in more detail in the section on managing debt.)

A familiar sight at a bank these days is the big, computerized cash machine outside. It's called an automated teller machine, or ATM. An ATM is open twenty-four hours a day, seven days a week. ATMs can be found at banks and are often located in stores and other places. It's a convenient way to withdraw or deposit money, especially when the bank itself is closed or you're not near the bank. You can even use ATMs in another city, another state, or a foreign country.

Contrary to how it might appear, money doesn't grow inside ATMs any more than it grows on trees. ATMs don't give out "free" money; they work like a checking or savings account, and most banks charge ATM users a small fee. Bank customers, using a special plastic card and a personal identification code, can make deposits or withdraw limited amounts of cash. Generally, you can't take out more cash than the amount you have deposited in your checking or savings account.

An ATM is one form of *electronic banking.* Banking by telephone or through home computers also is becoming increasingly popular. Electronic banking allows you to transfer money between accounts

or to check on your account balances. Computers let you get up-to-the-minute bank statements or even pay bills. Computer technology is making it possible to use special cash cards in place of cash and debit cards in place of checks. Changes in electronic banking might someday make checks and cash nearly obsolete.

While these changes will provide convenience and speed, they might also make it quite easy to spend money. Handing over cold cash or writing a check makes one think about what one is buying. Handing someone a plastic card, punching numbers on the telephone, or using a computer might make it extremely easy to overspend or borrow—and possibly to get into financial trouble.

Whatever form of banking you choose, shop around when you select a bank, just as you would at clothing or music stores. Banks charge different fees for checking accounts, pay different interest rates on savings and checking accounts, charge different interest rates for loans, and offer a variety of customer services.

Other Types of Financial Institutions

Unlike banks, most *savings and loan* institutions are owned by their customers. Originally, they were formed mainly to make home loans, but now they offer many other services similar to banks.

A *credit union* provides banking services only to a certain group of people with a common bond, such as employees who work for the same company.

Banks, savings and loans, and credit unions make up only one type of financial institution. You also might need to use an insurance company, a stock brokerage firm, or an accounting firm. Some of these firms provide services similar to those offered by banks, but many of their services are unique.

Some of the different types of professionals who provide financial help are listed on the next page. They may charge for their services by the hour, charge a set fee, be paid a percentage of the amount of money involved, or be paid by a combination of these ways.

- A *financial planner* is somewhat new in the financial world. Planners help people look at their current financial situation and identify their financial goals, and recommend ways to reach those goals. Many planners, through education and testing, obtain professional certification such as the CFP®, or Certified Financial Planner, license. Their recommendations may involve some or all of the other types of financial professionals.

- A *stockbroker* is licensed (has passed an exam) to sell stocks, bonds, and other types of investments to the public.

- An *insurance agent* must be licensed to sell auto, home, health, or other types of insurance.

- Traditionally, an *accountant* prepares tax returns and examines the financial records of businesses and individuals. Some accountants also provide financial planning services.

- A *tax preparer* calculates clients' taxes each year. Many tax preparers are accountants, but that is not a requirement.

- A licensed *real estate agent* helps customers find and buy or sell a home.

- People often think of an *attorney* only as someone who defends people accused of crimes. But many attorneys specialize in providing income tax advice, preparing legal documents that have financial consequences, and negotiating business deals.

8

Learning About Investing

You've learned about *saving* for a goal—that is, setting aside money for something you want to buy or do later. Maybe you once put quarters and dollar bills in your piggy bank for several weeks. That was saving. Then one day you emptied the bank and took the money to buy something. You also can save your money in a savings account at a bank or other financial institution.

For some larger goals, you should *invest* your money. A financial investment is something you put your money into with the purpose of getting more money back. An investment also can be one of time and labor. For example, you might invest in a lawn mower with the idea that you could make enough money mowing lawns over the summer to more than pay for the mower, gas, and maintenance.

You also are an investment. You can invest in yourself through education, for example, or by learning new skills or trades. Education and self-improvement can help you earn more income. In fact, of all the types of investments available, investing in yourself is the best investment you can make. It can pay big dividends.

Unlike saving in a bank account, investing implies there is a risk—that is, you are not *guaranteed* that you will actually earn more than the amount you invest. (The amount invested is called *principal.*) In fact, there is a chance that you won't get back all or even part of your principal. Some investments are riskier than others.

Investing is used to achieve certain types of goals. People typically *save* for short-term goals such as a new car or a family vacation. They put their money into something like a savings account, from which they are sure they can get all their money back soon, plus a little interest.

People *invest* for long-term goals like college or retirement. They invest in such things as stocks, bonds, or real estate, which do not guarantee either the principal invested or any earnings on the principal. However, because of these greater risks, investors have a chance to earn higher *returns* (income or an increase in value) than they would from a savings account, especially over a long period of time. In general, the greater the risk, the higher the potential reward (or loss); the lower the risk, the less money you'll earn (or lose).

There also is a difference between investing and *speculation.* Speculation is much like gambling. The chances that you will make money speculating are slim. In addition, chances that you will lose money are great. With a sound investment, the odds of making money usually are greater than they are of losing money.

Basic Types of Investments

Financial investments take two basic forms: owned investments or loaned investments. That is, you are either a lender or an owner.

A *loaned investment* means you loan money to a company or government in return for its promise to repay the principal (the amount you loaned), plus interest. Such an investment is similar to how you "loan" money to a bank through your savings account, except that, with an investment, there is only a *promise* to repay the money, not a guarantee. Most loaned investments are called "debt instruments" because the issuer is in debt to you. The issuer makes regular or "fixed" payments of income, often monthly, for a fixed length of time.

Common loaned investments include:

- Money market funds
- Certificates of deposit
- U.S. government bonds
- Corporate, municipal (city), and foreign bonds
- Annuities
- Cash-value life insurance

You might already own one form of loaned investment—U.S. Savings Bonds. These make popular gifts for families, grandparents, or others to buy for children because savings bonds can be bought in small amounts (as little as $25). Basically, savings bonds are a loan to the federal government. The government agrees to repay the bondholder the amount invested, with interest, after a set period of time. Governments or companies issue bonds to raise money for certain projects, such as building roads or factories.

Also popular are certificates of deposit (sometimes called time deposits) issued by banks. The investor lends the bank a specific amount of money for a specific period of time at a specific interest rate. In general, the longer the time, the higher the interest rate.

An *owned investment* means you actually own part or all of a company, real estate, or other asset. (An *asset* is an item of value.) You own the asset just as you might own a bike or your family owns a car. If you buy *stock* in a large fast-food restaurant chain, for example, you actually own part of the company (probably along with millions of other people). You get to share in any profits (or losses). If you own enough stock in a fast-food chain, you get to help run the company (and maybe even get free food).

It's easy to own stock, even for a teenager, although you must be at least age 18 or set up a special custodial account with your parents or guardian. Investors commonly buy at least one hundred shares of stock at a time, but some stockbrokers will let young people buy only a few shares of stock in a company. That can be helpful to you because a single share can cost anywhere from a few dollars to more than $100. Often you can buy a single share if you join an investment club. And some companies—generally those selling products that kids buy—will allow young people to buy a fraction of a single share directly from the company.

As a stockholder, you may receive *dividends* (profits the company pays to its stockholders). Dividends usually are issued quarterly, or every three months. However, unlike interest payments from loaned investments, dividends are not promised (a company can't guarantee how much profit it will make, if any).

You also can make money from an owned investment by selling the investment for more than you paid for it. An investor usually buys shares of stock, for example, in the hope that the stock's price will increase before the investor sells the shares. You might have done the same thing with a baseball card. Perhaps you paid $5 for a particular card and later sold it for $7. The $2 you made on the sale is a *profit,* sometimes called a *capital gain.*

Common types of owned investments include:

- Stock in U.S. and foreign companies
- Mutual fund shares
- Real estate (land, homes, farms, or office buildings)
- A personal business (like a hardware store)
- Gold, silver, and diamonds (commodities)
- Rare stamps, paintings, and other collectibles

There are experts who study how well a particular investment does compared with other investments. These experts typically look at the investment's yield, profit, and total return. An investment's *yield* is what the investment pays you directly in income. This might be in the form of interest (from bonds), dividends (from stocks), or rental income (from an apartment or office building). *Profit,* or capital gain, is discussed above. *Total return* is the combination of an investment's income and its profit (or loss). Total return tells the investor how much the investment actually made in dollars and cents over the entire time that the investor owned the asset.

Reducing Risk

Every investment carries some risk: the risk that you won't get all your original investment back, or that you won't make as much money as you expected. One of the best ways to reduce risk is to invest in several different types of investments. This is called *diversification.* You've probably heard the saying, "Don't put all your eggs in

one basket." That way, if you drop a "basket," you won't lose all of that day's "eggs." When investors spread their money among different types of investments, both loaned and owned investments, they avoid losing all of their money if one or two of the investments sour.

Mutual funds are one easy way to spread your investment eggs among many baskets. A mutual fund is a company that receives money from many investors (called shareholders). The fund then invests that money in stocks, bonds, or other types of assets. Any interest, dividends, or profits the fund earns are passed back to the investors, according to the number of shares they own, minus a small percentage that the fund keeps to pay its operating expenses and earn a profit.

A mutual fund is able to reduce risk because, by pooling money from shareholders, it can invest in many (sometimes more than a hundred) different stocks, bonds, or other types of investments. Then if (for example) a few stocks don't do well, the greater number of stocks that do perform well can more than make up for the losses. An individual investor would find it difficult to own that many different investments. It would cost too much and take too much time.

However, many mutual funds invest in only certain types of stocks (such as technology companies or banks) or certain types of bonds (government or corporate). Because of this, investors should further diversify their money by investing in more than one mutual fund.

You might not be able to invest in mutual funds right away. Most funds require a minimum investment of at least $250, and some require an investment of $1,000 or more. But once you open a mutual fund account, you usually can invest smaller amounts in the future. (You must be at least age 18, or use a custodial account.)

One inexpensive way to invest in a mutual fund is through an individual retirement account (IRA). An IRA is designed to help people save money to live on after they retire from their normal work life. An IRA is an investment account that receives special tax benefits from the government. This allows the investment to grow faster, so you have a bigger nest egg when you retire. You can open an IRA through a mutual fund for as little as $100.

Mutual funds have many advantages, but they still have some investment risk. Their shareholders can lose money, especially over a short time period. Over a long period, however, many mutual funds have excellent track records for making money for their shareholders.

The "Power" of Compounding

So what's the payoff for doing all this saving and investing? Is it really worth the effort? Why not just spend all of the money you earn now instead of investing some of it for use later?

Saving and investing do something special that earning money from a job cannot do: The money itself can earn more money. Simply stated, your money works for you, just as you work for your money. The ability of money to grow on its own can be extremely valuable in achieving long-term goals and in giving you financial security as you grow older.

If you go to your local bank, deposit $100 in a savings account, and don't touch that money for a year, what will happen? The bank will pay interest on that $100—say 5.25 percent a year. (Interest rates vary.) The bank is loaning out that money to other customers at a higher interest rate, which is how it makes money.

A bank can pay two kinds of interest: *simple* or *compound.* With simple interest at the rate of 5.25 percent a year, the bank would pay $5.25 at the end of the year for your deposit of $100. So you would have a total of $105.25 in your account. With compound interest, the interest is added to the principal throughout the year, and then interest is calculated on the larger principal amount. Basically, the bank is paying interest on the interest as well as on the initial deposit. Compounding interest daily (some banks compound only two or four times a year) would mean you would earn $5.39 instead of $5.25. That's not much of a difference, of course. But this example is based on a small amount of money for only one year.

The real "power" of compounding becomes clear over time. Imagine that the Native Americans who sold New York City's Manhattan Island to a Dutch trading company in 1626 had received $24 in cash instead of goods valued at $24. Also imagine that they had put that cash into a savings account earning 5 percent a year and left it alone all these years. Today, their $24 would have grown to more than $1.66 billion. Imagine what $100 would have earned over that time!

Obviously, you don't have more than three hundred seventy years to wait for your money to grow. But you can still watch it grow pretty fast.

Imagine that you have invested $100 in one of the types of investments discussed earlier. Suppose the investment earns 10 percent each year. At the end of the first year, the total investment will be worth $110.

If you spend the $10 you made and leave the $100 invested, you'll have $110 at the end of the second year. If you do this each year for ten years, your $100 investment will have earned a total of $100 (all of which you've spent).

But consider what would happen if you didn't spend the first $10 earned. Instead, you leave it with the original $100. Then the next year's interest is based on a principal of $110, not $100. At the end of the second year, your investment will have earned $11 and the total will have grown to $121. Again, you reinvest your earnings, and earn 10 percent on a principal of $121 instead of on a principal of only $100 (as in the first example).

Do this for ten years and the investment will have earned $159.39—nearly $60 more than in the first example. What's more, the investment's total value will have grown to $259.39, compared with the $100 total value in the example where you spent your earnings each year. That's the marvel of money earning money.

Compounding

Year	Spend earnings	Reinvest earnings
1	$ 10	$ 10.00
2	$ 10	$ 11.00
3	$ 10	$ 12.10
4	$ 10	$ 13.31
5	$ 10	$ 14.64
6	$ 10	$ 16.11
7	$ 10	$ 17.72
8	$ 10	$ 19.49
9	$ 10	$ 21.44
10	$ 10	$ 23.58
Total earnings	$100	$159.39

Notice in the example above that the greatest earnings come in the later years. That's why compounding makes such a dramatic difference over time. Note that in the final two years, the "reinvest earnings" column shows more than twice the amount as the "spend earnings" column. In fact, if you extended the example just two more years, the reinvested earnings column would show $28.53, or almost three times as much as spent earnings.

Remember, too, that if you hadn't put the $100 in the bank in the first place, you would have earned absolutely nothing.

Still not convinced? Suppose someone agreed either to give you $10,000 or to double your money every day for thirty days, starting with only a penny. Which would you choose? The $10,000 sounds enticing. However, doubling your money every day for thirty days would make that penny grow to $10,737,417!

That's why it is important to start saving and investing regularly as a teenager. Even small amounts can make a difference. You won't double your money as fast as in the penny example, but the money you invest will grow faster than you think. (An investment earning 10 percent a year will double in value in only 7.2 years.)

Remember the IRA mentioned earlier—that special investment account for saving for retirement? Suppose you begin investing in an IRA at age 22. You put in the same amount of money each year for nine years, until you're 30, and then stop. You never invest another dime in that IRA. Instead, you let the money grow by itself.

Now imagine that a friend your age puts an identical amount of money each year into his IRA account, but he doesn't start until age 31. However, he puts in that amount of money each year for 35 years. When both of you reach age 65, which one will have more money? Check the accompanying chart. You might be surprised at the results.

How Money Grows Over Time*

(Note: The rate of interest in this example is 9 percent.)

Age	Contributions Made Early		Age	Contributions Made Later	
22	$2,000		22	$ 0	
23	2,000		23	0	
24	2,000	**Total**	24	0	
25	2,000	**of**	25	0	
26	2,000	**$18,000**	26	0	
27	2,000	**Invested**	27	0	
28	2,000		28	0	
29	2,000		29	0	
30	2,000		30	0	
31	0		31	2,000	
32	0		32	2,000	
33	0		33	2,000	
34	0		34	2,000	
35	0		35	2,000	
36	0		36	2,000	
37	0		37	2,000	
38	0		38	2,000	
39	0		39	2,000	
40	0		40	2,000	
41	0		41	2,000	
42	0		42	2,000	
43	0		43	2,000	**Total**
44	0		44	2,000	**of**
45	0		45	2,000	**$70,000**
46	0		46	2,000	**Invested**
47	0		47	2,000	
48	0		48	2,000	
49	0		49	2,000	
50	0		50	2,000	
51	0		51	2,000	
52	0		52	2,000	
53	0		53	2,000	
54	0		54	2,000	
55	0		55	2,000	
56	0		56	2,000	
57	0		57	2,000	
58	0		58	2,000	
59	0		59	2,000	
60	0		60	2,000	
61	0		61	2,000	
62	0		62	2,000	
63	0		63	2,000	
64	0		64	2,000	
65	0		65	2,000	

Amount available at age **65**: **$579,471**   **$470,249**

*Used with permission from the National Endowment for Financial Education®

9

Learning About Managing Debt

Imagine that you've had your eye on something you want to buy—new athletic shoes or a video game, for example. You've been saving up for it, but don't have enough money yet. Then one day you see the item on sale. It's a really good sale, but the sale is going to last only one week and there's no way you will have enough money saved before the sale is over.

You have two choices. First, you could continue to save your money until you can afford to buy the item. Many people must do this. You can't always buy something whenever you want it, even if it's on sale.

The second choice is to buy the item on credit. *Credit* is when you buy something now and pay for it later. Credit is based on trust. The person or company trusts that you will pay what you owe.

Credit is essentially a *loan*. You've probably had friends loan you a dollar to buy an ice-cream cone when you didn't have any money with you. You paid them back soon, maybe even the same day. Perhaps your parents have borrowed money from you because they didn't have enough cash with them to pay the baby-sitter or the pizza delivery person. They probably paid you back right away, too.

Borrowing from a friend or your parents usually is pretty straight-forward. You repay exactly the amount they loaned you. You might pay it back all at once or in several regular payments, called *installments*. If you borrow $10, for example, you might repay it over a month at $2.50 a week.

At some point, however, you'll probably need to take out a loan for which you pay back the amount you borrowed (the principal) plus a finance charge (or interest). Lenders, such as banks, charge borrowers for the privilege of temporarily using the lenders' money. (Remember, the bank pays interest on your savings account because you are letting the bank use your money.)

The total finance charge you pay depends on four basic factors:

1. The amount you borrow.
2. The amount of any fees charged by the lender.
3. The interest rate charged, which is generally a percentage of the principal. For example, if you borrow $10 at 5 percent interest, you would pay back the $10 plus 50 cents.
4. How long it takes you to pay back the loan.

Naturally, it's usually better not to borrow. Paying finance charges adds to the real cost of the item you are buying. But sometimes it's difficult to save enough ahead of time, especially for expensive items like a home, car, or college education.

If you decide to borrow, here are some tips to reduce your costs.

- Shop around. Different lenders charge different interest rates.

- Compare the *annual percentage rate* (APR), not just the stated interest rate. The APR reflects the true percentage rate of a loan because it takes into account various fees and other costs over a year. The APR is always higher than the simple interest rate on a loan.

- Ask what the total cost of the loan will be in dollars and cents. The lender is required to disclose this.

- Find out the amount of all fees. Fees add up quickly and can substantially increase the cost of a loan.

- Don't always choose the loan with the lowest payment. A lower payment may mean a longer payment period. The longer you take to repay a loan, the more you will pay in total interest charges. If you take five years to pay off a car loan instead of three, you'll pay nearly 60 percent more in interest.

Of course, the lender will check you out just as you should check out the lender. The lender must be confident that you can repay the loan. (Do you know people you wouldn't feel confident lending money to?) You probably will need to prove that you have steady income from a job and, if you've borrowed money before, that you paid it back. The lender may also ask for references—your employer or others who will state that you are trustworthy.

In some cases, a loan is "secured." This means the lender can take possession of whatever you bought with the money you borrowed, such as a car or a house, if you fail to make payments.

Plastic Money

"Plastic money" is a phrase commonly used for credit cards, those plastic cards people carry in their wallets. Unfortunately, the phrase reinforces the belief in some people's minds that credit cards are not real money. This belief probably explains why so many people get into financial difficulties using credit cards.

A credit card represents real money. A credit card is a form of a loan—just as if you borrowed cash from a bank. In fact, it's usually banks that issue credit cards. When you use a credit card to buy something (a process called *charging*), the store first checks electronically to make sure your credit is good. Then it gives you a slip of paper to sign, which is your agreement to repay the loan. The store is soon paid by the bank that issued the credit card, and the bank then collects the cost of the purchase from you.

A credit card can be a convenient substitute for carrying checks or a large amount of cash, and can be especially useful in an emergency. You can pay off the loan at your own pace, although you always have to pay at least a minimum amount each month. However, if you don't pay off the entire cost of what you bought when you receive the credit-card bill, you will pay a finance charge on the unpaid balance.

Some credit cards charge interest of 18 percent a year, or more. Imagine that you charge an item in January and take all year to pay it off. If your credit card charges 18 percent, you would end up paying 18 percent more for the item than if you had paid cash for it or had immediately paid off the total amount charged.

Credit cards have a charge limit, which means you can charge only up to the amount the credit-card issuer allows. This limit is usually based on your income, credit history, and other factors that might affect your ability to repay. When you reach your credit limit, you must stop charging more purchases until you pay off at least some of the accumulated debt.

There are several types of so-called "credit cards":

- A *debit card* works like a check. The amount is electronically deducted (debited) from your checking account and paid into the store's bank account.

- A *charge card* typically is restricted to purchases from a particular company, like a department store or a gasoline company. Most charge cards are like a credit card in that you don't have to pay off all of your charges, or your entire balance, at one time.

- A *credit card,* issued by a bank, can be used to pay for any product as long as the seller accepts the card. Not all sellers do.

By your late teens, you'll probably start receiving numerous offers from credit card companies to apply for their cards (especially if you attend college). Just remember that you are personally responsible and legally obligated to pay back all amounts charged to your card.

Credit Record

How responsibly you use a credit card, or any other form of credit such as a loan, will be reflected on your "credit record." A credit record is a history of how well you've paid your bills. Companies called *credit bureaus* keep track of the credit histories of individuals. Anyone extending credit to you will likely check with credit bureaus to see if you have paid your bills on time.

People who don't use credit responsibly can get into serious debt. They may owe more than they can reasonably pay back. If this happens to you, you might not be given further credit. Some auto insurers refuse coverage to drivers with bad credit histories. And other businesses, including potential employers, check credit histories. So it pays to maintain a good credit history by paying your debts on time.

If you do get into debt problems, here are some tips to help you reduce or eliminate debt:

- Reduce expenses. Stop buying things you don't need, such as fancy clothes, videos, or concert tickets.

- Don't charge anything. Pay cash. Many people find it harder to spend "real" money.

- Perform "plastic surgery." Cut up your credit cards if you can't stop yourself from using them.

- Make a spending plan, as you did earlier, to see where your money is coming in and exactly where it is going out.

- Earn extra money to pay off debts.

10

Controlling Risk

All of us face risks in life. Risk that we might become sick or hurt. Risk that something we own might be lost or destroyed. Risk that we might hurt others or their property. Risk that we might die and leave others in a difficult financial situation.

Risk management is the various ways people protect themselves against risks, especially those that can cause serious financial loss. In general, there are five ways to manage risk:

- **Avoid it.** To avoid the potential risks of driving a car, for example, you might take the bus.

- **Reduce it.** Taking a driver's education course and wearing a seat belt reduce the chances of serious injury or death from an auto accident. Locking or storing away your bike reduces the chance of theft.

- **Retain it.** This is sometimes inaccurately called self-insurance. You pay out of your own pocket for any loss or damage. People usually do this with less expensive items.

- **Transfer it.** When people can't avoid, reduce, or pay for financial loss themselves, they can transfer the financial risk to someone else. Transferring risk typically is done through the use of *insurance.* Insuring is paying an insurance company money (called premiums) for a guarantee that the company will pay for a financial loss suffered, particularly a major loss.

- **Share it.** When people own a business, they might want to limit the amount they could lose if the business failed. If the business is incorporated (turned into a corporation), the most the owners could lose is the amount they have invested in the business, represented by the shares of stock they own. If they didn't incorporate a business that they owned, the failure of the business might cost the owners everything they have.

How Insurance Works

People generally find that buying insurance is more affordable than trying to retain (pay out of pocket for) every risk. The idea behind insurance is that the risk—and thus the cost—is spread out over many people also insured by the company.

Set up an imaginary insurance fund to see how it works. Assume that all the students at your school ride their bikes to school each day. Over the course of the school year some of those bicycles, unfortunately, will be stolen and never recovered. If there are five hundred students, and each student puts $5 into a bicycle insurance fund, there will be a total of $2,500 in the fund.

Assume that each bike is worth $150. For each bicycle stolen (and not recovered), the fund pays the bicycle's owner $150—enough to buy a new bike. The money in the fund could be deposited in a bank account, where it would earn interest until it was needed.

Most students probably will not have their bikes stolen during the year (especially if they carefully lock their bikes). But for a mere $5 premium, they know that if their bicycle is stolen they won't have to go without a bike or pay $150 out of their own pocket to replace it.

That's a funny thing about insurance. It's something you pay for but hope you never have to use.

Insurance works on the basis of "odds"—the chance that something will happen that will cause the insurance company to pay for a loss. In the example above, as long as no more than sixteen bikes are stolen during the year, there will be enough money in the fund to cover all the losses. Real insurance companies use a long history of experience to determine the odds that someone will have an auto accident or that a home might be damaged by fire or that someone will die. By knowing the odds and the cost of replacing a loss, the company sets the amount of premium to charge its customers.

Types of Insurance

You are probably still too young to have any real need for most types of insurance. On the other hand, if you are old enough to drive, you've already encountered one major type of insurance—automobile insurance.

Here is a review of six of the most common types of insurance and why you might need them—if not now, perhaps soon after you start living on your own.

1. **Automobile insurance.** The chances that a teenager will be involved in an auto accident within the first five years behind the wheel are 75 percent. No wonder auto insurance is more expensive for teenagers than for adults. Insurance companies charge more to insure teenagers because statistics show that they are more likely than more experienced drivers to get into accidents.

   Auto insurance generally will pay for damage to your car and to other cars involved if the accident is your fault. Insurance also usually covers medical payments if you or others are injured. Auto liability insurance is the only type of insurance required by law. Of course, if you don't own or drive a car, you won't need this insurance.

2. **Insurance for homeowners/renters (property insurance).** You might not own a home for a while, but you'll probably rent an apartment or a house early in your adult life. Renter's insurance pays for the replacement of personal possessions damaged or destroyed in, or stolen from, an apartment or a rented home.

3. **Medical insurance.** People of all ages are at risk of becoming ill or injured seriously enough to require medical care such as

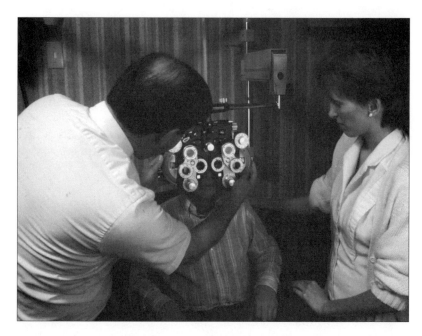

surgery or hospitalization. Medical care is expensive. Health insurance can cover most of the costs, especially major bills that could be financially devastating to an individual or a family. Employers often provide medical insurance. If your employer doesn't, or if you are self-employed, you might need to buy medical insurance on your own.

4. **Life insurance.** Life insurance pays a specific sum of money to selected people (beneficiaries) when the person who is insured dies. The amount of this payout, called a death benefit, depends on the size of the premiums paid each year.

The most common purpose of life insurance is to provide income to people who depend on you financially. You probably don't need life insurance yet. But when you are old enough to raise a family, or if someday other people such as aunts, grandparents, or your parents depend on you financially, you probably should have life insurance.

There are many different types of life insurance, but they fall into two general categories:

Term life insurance sounds like what it is—you buy coverage for only a certain term, or period of time, such as five years. If you renew the insurance at the end of that time, you pay higher annual premiums because you are older and chances are higher that you may die. Term is the least expensive type of life insurance because you are paying only for the cost of the death benefit. It's especially affordable for people with limited income or who have several people depending on them financially.

Permanent life insurance provides a death benefit, just like term insurance. But part of the annual premium is invested in a "cash value" account where the money can grow free of current taxes. (You can borrow or take money out of the account.) The annual premiums initially are more expensive than the premiums you would pay for a similar amount of term insurance. However, the premiums may be guaranteed never to go up for as long as you live, and you remain insured for as long as you pay the premiums. Permanent life insurance comes in several forms. The most common is whole life insurance. Some other forms are called universal life insurance, variable life insurance, variable universal life insurance, adjustable life insurance, and indeterminate premium life insurance.

5. **Disability insurance.** As explained earlier, people buy insurance to protect themselves against possible financial loss. One of your greatest financial assets is your ability to earn money. If you're disabled by an accident or illness, you might not be able to continue working, and your income would stop. Disability insurance would replace most, but not all, of the income you would lose if you were unable to work. Unfortunately, many people overlook buying this kind of insurance.

6. **Liability insurance.** Personal responsibility—being responsible for yourself—carries some risk with it. Sometimes courts hold an individual legally responsible for what happens to someone else. For example, if you don't shovel the snow from your sidewalk and someone slips on it, that person might sue you for the medical costs of his or her injuries. Liability insurance pays for those costs if you are found to be legally responsible. The portion of auto insurance required by law is also a form of liability insurance.

11

Planning Your Time

How many times have you heard someone tell you to "stop wasting your time"?

Sure, it's fun to "waste time"—to sleep late, watch TV, or just hang around with friends. It's okay to do that, just as it's okay to spend some money on fun things. Life doesn't have to be completely serious.

But spending your time unwisely becomes a serious situation if you waste time to a point where it prevents you from doing other things that you really need or want to do. If you spend too much time in front of the TV, you won't get your homework done or you won't be prepared to go on the Scout trip. If you put off doing your chores, then you might not be able to go somewhere with a friend.

It is important to remember one special thing about time: You can't get it back. Once it's gone, it's gone forever. You can lose money on a bad investment and make it up by earning extra money, if necessary. But you can't earn extra time. You can't save time to use later, trade it with someone else, or buy it back. Each of us is given the same amount of time each day, and we get to spend it as we choose. If we choose to spend it wisely, it pays dividends—just like an investment.

So it's important to learn to manage time just as you've learned to manage money—carefully and with thought. Remember, you're learning how to take more responsibility for yourself, and managing your time is one important way of taking control and accepting responsibility for yourself.

Setting Goals

Remember how you set goals to better manage your money? You also can set goals for using time wisely. When you were younger, you probably felt you "had more time" than you do today. You didn't, of course. You had the same number of hours in the day as you do now. You just didn't have so many things to do in those hours.

A key to making the most of the time you have is to set goals and plan the activities you want or need to do to accomplish those goals. What must be done, and what can wait? The answers to these questions will go a long way toward helping you use your time effectively.

Just as with financial goals, there are two basic types of time-management goals: short-term and long-term.

Short-term goals are those things you want or need to do today, tomorrow, or in the next few days. They might include going to baseball practice or a troop meeting, finishing a homework assignment, or washing the family car.

Long-term goals are things you want to accomplish over the next several weeks, months, or even years. Perhaps you need to write a term paper, want to earn two or three merit badges, or would like to learn to play a musical instrument.

Do what you did with your financial goals: Write down your short-term goals and your long-term goals. Be specific about *what* you want to do (which two merit badges to complete, for example); *when* you will do it (in how many days, weeks, or months); *how long* it will take (number of hours); and *how* you are going to accomplish it (set aside two hours each weekend, for instance).

It's important to write down goals—that way they stick in your mind better. List your long-term goals on a piece of paper. Pin the list to a bulletin board or some other prominent location in your room as a permanent reminder.

On a calendar or other daily organizer, list activities that are more immediate. This is your "to do" list. Today, for example, you might need to read a chapter for history class, go to soccer practice from 4:00 to 5:30 P.M., and practice your trombone for thirty minutes.

Don't limit your choice of goals and activities just yet. Write them all down. Then use the next section to help you figure out which ones deserve more of your time.

Setting Priorities

Life is full of activities. Most people have more things to do than time in which to do them. That's especially true in today's fast-paced society. People in Scouting tend to be active and involved. They like "doing things." Besides Scouting, you might be involved in sports, band, or the drama club. You might have a part-time job. And there's all that homework to do. Your Scout leaders also are busy people— they might have full-time jobs, families, or be involved in sports, church, and other community activities. Whew! Life can get hectic.

Because most people don't have time to do everything they need and want to do, it's important to set priorities. Some things will be obvious: doing homework, going to Scout meetings or church, getting to work on time. Whether other things are important might be less clear. Maybe you have a plastic model you want to assemble, you want to improve your batting so you can make the baseball team, and there are two merit badges you want to earn in the next three months. But you might not have time to do all three things. Which one is most important to you? Which one is least important?

Go down both your short-term list and your long-term list and ask, "Do I really want (or need) to do this activity?" Mark the most important item with a 1. Put a 2 beside the second most important, and so on, until you have numbered each item in order by priority. Then simply work on the most important items first.

Accomplishing Goals

Now you have your list of things to do, ranked in order of importance. But how do you get started? Getting started can be the hardest part. That's why some call *procrastination*, or putting things off, the "thief of time."

People are more likely to procrastinate when a project is large or unpleasant or the deadline is a long time away. One trick is to break a large project or goal into stages, with a deadline for each stage. Imagine that you have a major term paper to write for a history class, and it's due in six weeks. Instead of putting only the due date on your calendar, break the term paper into stages:

- Collect research materials
- Take notes on research materials
- Organize notes and write an outline
- Write first draft
- Write second draft
- Prepare final copy

Set a deadline for each stage and write those deadlines on your calendar. You might collect research materials this week, take notes the following week, and so on. That way, the term paper becomes several smaller, easier tasks instead of one large, difficult project.

Remember the example of the IRA and the value of investing money earlier compared with investing it later? When you're young, retirement seems a long way off. Young people find it easy to put off

saving for retirement because they think they have so much time. Yet suddenly (it seems sudden, anyway), a person is nearly retired and realizes that he or she didn't put aside any savings all those years. Remember, you can't go back in time. Time is lost forever. You can, however, avoid "wasting" many years by breaking down a far-away goal (saving a nest egg for retirement) into minigoals (saving X dollars this year, XX dollars next year, and so on). Then the task no longer seems so overwhelming.

Time Tips

- Reward yourself for accomplishments along the way. Tell yourself you will get a snack, shoot a few baskets, or just relax for a few minutes *after* you finish a particular homework assignment or a chore at home.

- Schedule some "waste" time each day. Don't become a "time nut," always watching the clock and filling every minute of the day with a task. Allow yourself time to relax, watch a little TV, read, or "do nothing."

- Schedule "emergency" time. Life rarely goes according to plan. Things often take longer than you planned, or unexpected things happen. When you schedule your day, leave a cushion of time as a backup to use in case you get behind.

- Check off each item as you complete it to mark your progress. This is especially useful when you break down a large project into stages.

- Try to schedule the toughest tasks for the time of day when you're most productive. Are you a "morning" or "evening" person?

- Be flexible. Make adjustments if necessary.

- Ask for help or directions. It can save much time.

- Eliminate low-priority items. Ask yourself, "What don't I have to do?" as often as you ask, "What do I have to do?"

- Say no. Commit yourself only to things you must do or you really want to do.

- Stop often and ask, "What's the best use of my time right now?"

- Reevaluate (rethink) your goals from time to time.

12

Thinking About Your Future

You've probably thought about what you'd like to do for a living when you're an adult. Perhaps you've dreamed of being a professional athlete, musician, military pilot, truck driver, teacher, police officer, or auto mechanic, or the president of your own company. These are careers—your life's work.

A job is not a career. You might have a job mowing lawns during the summer, but you might not want to make that your career (although some people do—lawn mowing and maintenance services can be profitable and satisfying). A job can be part of a career, as a specific place where you work to fulfill some of your career goals. A professional basketball player, for example, might hold several "jobs"— that is, play for several different teams—during his basketball career. Experts say that, on average, people go through ten different jobs and three different careers during their working lives.

A career is a way to earn money. You are paid money for performing certain duties. But a career should be more than just a way to make a living. Ideally, it should be emotionally, spiritually, and intellectually satisfying as well. You should try to choose a career that you truly like and that you're good at. It can be tough working in a job you don't like, even if you're making a good living.

Exploring Career Possibilities

You might not have thought seriously about what career you'd like to have when you're an adult. That's okay. It's difficult to know something like that when you're young. Or you might already be getting serious about what you want to do, especially if you are nearing graduation from high school. In either case, you can do a number of things to explore potential careers.

1. Think about your interests and hobbies. What excites you? A fascination with rocks might suggest a career in geology. If you enjoy working with people, you could become a teacher or a sales representative. Like to work with your hands? How about becoming a carpenter or an artist?

2. Consider what things you do well. For example, strong math skills might suggest a career as an accountant, an engineer, or a scientist.

3. Talk to people who work in careers you're interested in. Visit them at work, if possible. Watch what they do and notice their working conditions. What hours do they work? Ask what they like about their work, and what they don't like. What skills did they need to acquire (math, writing, communication skills)?

4. Do research at the library. Many books are available that describe different jobs and what's involved.

5. Write for information. People who do similar jobs often band together in trade or professional associations. These groups can be good sources of career information.

6. Attend job and career fairs. Companies send representatives to these fairs to discuss job and career opportunities. Your school is a good source for job-fair information.

7. Find out how well the career pays. Money isn't everything, but you'll want to make a comfortable living with your career.

8. Consider whether job opportunities in the career are growing. Some careers, especially those requiring special skills or education, offer more opportunities than others. Is it a lifetime career? If you're lucky enough, being a major-league baseball player may be a great career, but what will you do when you can no longer play?

9. Find out what education or licensing is required. Do you need to go to college or a vocational school? Some jobs require licenses. In other jobs, you might be able to learn at the workplace as an apprentice.

10. Determine where the jobs are. Some jobs are found only in large cities or certain locations.

11. Join an Explorer post. Many Explorer posts focus on a specific career area such as law enforcement or maritime (commercial shipping) work. Contact your BSA local council to find out if there is an Explorer post in your community that focuses on a career you're interested in.

12. Get a summer or part-time job or do volunteer work in an area that's related to the career you're thinking about. Such experiences, sometimes called internships, can be valuable in helping you to choose a career. This practical work experience may also improve your chances of getting a specific job when you actually start your career.

13. Begin to build your résumé. A *résumé* is a brief history of your work experience that you give to a potential employer when you are seeking work. List your paying jobs and community or volunteer work, as well as accomplishments such as making the school honor roll, serving as editor of the school newspaper, or serving in leadership positions in Scouting. All of these factors help an employer decide whether you're the right person for the job.

Education . . . Who Needs It?

Some days it probably is a little tough sitting in school. Maybe you want to get out into the work world and start earning some "real" money. But hold on. Before you skip out or skimp on your education, think about what it's going to cost you. Sure, you can make some money in the short run while your classmates are sitting in school. But in the long run, they will come out ahead financially—way ahead.

According to U.S. Census Bureau figures, a high school graduate, on average, makes 60 percent more than someone who doesn't have a high school diploma. And a graduate from a four-year college earns nearly twice what a high school graduate earns, and three times what a high school dropout earns. If you go on to get a professional degree, such as in law or medicine, you'll earn, on average, about *six* times what you would have earned if you had dropped out of high school.

You don't have to choose a career right away. In fact, it's probably best to explore several career possibilities to find the one that's right for you. A career is a big part of a person's everyday life. It's important to spend that time doing something you truly enjoy and find worthwhile.

Finding a rewarding career takes thought, creativity, and hard work. It means setting specific goals for where you want to be in five, ten, and twenty years. It means investing in yourself, by staying in school or perhaps through retraining or going back to school. It means taking responsibility for your own future.

Glossary

An **asset** is something you own or possess that has value. Assets can be personal or financial.

A **bank** is a financial institution that holds people's money for safe-keeping, pays interest on it, processes checks, and provides services such as loans, safe-deposit boxes, and investment services.

Bartering is exchanging, or trading, goods or services.

A **budget** is a spending/savings plan that shows what income you receive, how you plan to spend it, and how you actually spend it.

Capital gain, or profit, is the increase in the value of an asset between the time the asset is bought and the time it's sold.

A **checking account** is a bank account that checks can be written against; a check tells the bank how much money to take out of the account and pay to the person or company (the payee) to whom the check is written.

Compound interest is interest paid or computed on the principal amount, plus the interest that the principal has earned previously and that has been left in the account.

Buying on **credit** means buying an item now but paying for it later.

A **credit union** is a financial institution that provides banking services only to a certain group of people with a common bond, such as employees who work for the same company.

A **debit card** is a card (usually made of plastic) by which money can be withdrawn or the cost of purchases can be paid for directly from the cardholder's bank account.

Debt is something owed to someone; it includes an obligation to pay back what is owed.

To **deposit** money means to put money into a financial account, such as a checking or savings account.

Discretionary income is income you can spend as you choose; it does not have to be spent to pay debts or meet expenses.

Diversification means putting money into several different investments.

Dividends are profits a company pays to the people who own shares or "pieces" of the company.

Electronic banking is banking by telephone, home computer, or automated teller machine (ATM).

A **goal** is a specific purpose or destination.

Income is money a person or family receives that can be spent. Income might come from a job, an allowance, or gifts.

Interest is a charge for borrowing money. A bank pays you interest when it "borrows" the money in your savings account to lend to others; likewise, you pay a bank interest when you borrow money from it.

A financial **investment** is something people put money into with the goal of getting even more money back.

A **loan** is money given for temporary use, on the condition that it be repaid, usually with interest.

A **loaned investment** means loaning money to a company or government in return for its promise to repay the principal, plus interest.

Needs are the things people must have to survive, such as food, clothing, shelter, and medical care.

Objectives are the steps or tasks to be accomplished to reach a goal.

To **overdraw** a financial account means to draw (write) checks on the account for more money than is in it; being overdrawn means having an overdrawn account.

An **owned investment** means the investor actually owns part or all of a company, real estate, or other asset.

Personal management is being responsible for yourself, your money, your time, and your future.

Principal is the basic amount of money invested, or the basic amount of money due as a debt.

A financial **profit** is an increase in value.

A **résumé** is a summary of a person's work experience and career-related accomplishments.

Retirement generally occurs when a person concludes his or her normal working life, usually at an older age.

A **return** on an investment is the profit from or increase in value of the investment; total return is the combination of an investment's yield and its profit (or loss).

Risk management refers to the various ways (such as insurance and incorporation) by which people protect themselves against risks, especially risks that can cause serious financial loss.

A **savings account** is a bank account that earns interest, and that usually requires written authorization on a special form before withdrawals can be made.

A **savings and loan** is a financial association that holds and pays interest on the savings of its members, and invests mainly in home mortgage loans.

Simple interest is interest paid or computed only on the original principal of a loan or the beginning amount in an account.

Owning **stock** in a company means owning a part or share of the company.

Take-home pay is the money left from a paycheck after an employer has taken deductions for taxes, Social Security, and other items such as health insurance; it's the money the worker "takes home."

Utilities are water, gas, and electricity. Sometimes these are included in the cost of rent, sometimes not.

Wants are the things people desire to make life more comfortable or pleasant, but don't necessarily need for survival.

To **withdraw** money means to take money out of a financial account.

Yield is what an investment pays directly in income; yield might be in the form of interest, dividends, or rental income from property.

Resources on Personal Management

Scouting Literature

American Business, American Labor, Family Life, Salesmanship, and *Scholarship* merit badge pamphlets; see also merit badge pamphlets on particular careers or vocations.

Books and Other Publications

Berg, Adriane G., and Arthur B. Bochner. *The Totally Awesome Money Book for Kids and Their Parents.* Newmarket Press, 1993.

Bodnar, Janet. *Kiplinger's Money-Smart Kids: And Parents, Too!* Kiplinger Books, 1993.

Federal Trade Commission. "The Real Deal." 1995.

Houser, Peggy, and Hassell Bradley. *How to Teach Children About Money.* Western Freelance Writing Services, Ltd., 1989.

Morris, Kenneth M. *The Wall Street Journal Guide to Understanding Personal Finance.* Simon & Schuster Trade, 1993.

———. *The Wall Street Journal Guide to Money and Investing.* Simon & Schuster Trade, 1994.

National Endowment for Financial Education Academic Staff. *High School Financial Planning Program Student Workbook.* NEFE, 1992.

Acknowledgments

This new edition of the *Personal Management* merit badge pamphlet was written by Brent A. Neiser, CFP, director of the Public Education Center of the Denver-based National Endowment for Financial Education® (NEFE®). The National Endowment for Financial Education®, NEFE®, and the NEFE logo are federally registered service marks of the National Endowment for Financial Education. NEFE is an independent, nonprofit educational organization dedicated to improving the financial well-being of Americans. CFP and Certified Financial Planner are federally registered service marks of the Certified Financial Planner Board of Standards Inc.

NATIONAL ENDOWMENT FOR FINANCIAL EDUCATION

Photo Credits

Doug Knutson—page 60
National Endowment for Financial Education®/David Muenker—
    pages 8, 10, 16, 26, 30, 38, and 43
Randy Piland—pages 22, 35, 50, 56, 58, 62, 68, and 69
Doug Wilson—page 15

NOTES